P9-DVU-516

D0037850

THE

# GRANNY

**an insider's guide for new grandmothers**

# DIARIES

*by* Adair Lara

**ILLUSTRATIONS** *by* **PATRICIA STORMS**

**CHRONICLE BOOKS**
SAN FRANCISCO

Text copyright
© 2008 *by* **ADAIR LARA**

Illustrations copyright
© 2008 *by* **PATRICIA STORMS**

Library of Congress Cataloging-in-
Publication Data:

Lara, Adair.
 The Granny diaries / by Adair Lara ;
illustrations by Patricia Storms.
   p. cm.
  ISBN: 978-0-8118-5732-1
1. Grandmothers—Humor.
2. Grandparenting—Humor.  I. Title.

   HQ759.9.L37 2008
   649'.10853—DC22

      2007027413

Manufactured in China

Design *by* **JAY PETER SALVAS**
This book was typeset in Adobe
   Caslon 11.25/15 and Gotham 9.5/15

10 9 8 7 6 5 4 3 2 1

Chronicle Books LLC
  680 Second Street
  San Francisco, California 94107

WWW.CHRONICLEBOOKS.COM

## ACKNOWLEDGMENTS

I want especially to thank my daughter, Morgan, for giving me grandchildren so fast, and for letting me write about them, and Ryan and Maggie for changing me from a self-respecting detached and ironic adult into a love-struck grandmother who carries in her purse a tiny Phillips-head screwdriver just for installing batteries in toys. I want to thank my co-grandmother, Barbara Anderson, for being such a good sport about my remarks on paternal grandmothers. I also want to thank my friend Linda Kilby for her stories and my editors at Chronicle Books, Kate Prouty and Jodi Warshaw, for able and deft editing. I want to thank my mother, Lee Daly, and my mother-in-law, Shirley LeBlond, for showing me how to be a grandmother. And my husband, Bill LeBlond, for taking this journey with me.

*All that matters is what we do for each other.* —Lewis Carroll

*The reason grandchildren and grandparents get along so well is that they have a common enemy.* —Sam Levenson

# TABLE OF
# Contents

PART **1**

BECOMING A
**Grandmother**

# Birth

I was in the labor and delivery room at Kaiser Foundation Hospital on Geary Boulevard in San Francisco. My daughter Morgan, twenty-four, and her soon-to-be husband, Trevor, twenty-six, were about to produce a miracle, a small and tender human being who would need bathing, onesies, all-terrain strollers, instruction in voting, and—a grandmother.

I was so full of feelings: grateful to be there, proud of Morgan, pumped up with my own status as the mother of the most important person in the room, and, above all, eager to meet the baby. Morgan had said that everybody had to leave when the baby came—she wanted only Trevor in the room (and the ten or fifteen hospital staffers who wandered in and out). "But people can come and go during labor," she added kindly.

My head whipped around.
*"People?"*
It's a new shock to be called "people" by someone you have given birth to. But I said nothing. I had decided to be an exemplary, noninterfering

grandmother. Here was my first opportunity to display my tact. "Of course, sweetie," I said.

Morgan was attached to a fetal monitor that showed not only her contractions and the baby's heartbeat but also those of the women in three other rooms. "It's like watching a horse race," said Bob, Trevor's dad. He and Trevor's mother, Barbara, had hurried down from Davis, an hour east of San Francisco, to wait with the rest of us. Barbara stitched on a baby quilt in the corner, and Bob paced. Jim, my ex and Morgan's dad, came in and out, bringing Trivial Pursuit cards, Morgan's constitutional law textbook, a fresh T-shirt for Trevor, and whatever else the kids had decided they needed from home. Bill, my husband, was out in the hall with three days' worth of *New York Times*.

The doctor came in. It was almost time. The other three grandparents went outside to join Bill. "Should I go?" I muttered to Morgan, and she shook her sweaty head—I should stay. *Yes!* I exulted. I felt guilty staying when the others went out—but how could I miss this? Besides, Morgan might need me.

It was time for her to push. My arm aching, I lifted Morgan's head, pillow and all, to help her bury it in her breastbone. (The labor nurse said it would help her push the baby out.) Trevor was on her other side, wearing the Hughes Construction baseball hat that never left his head. He'd refused to leave the room, even to move their Subaru from the red zone he'd left it in.

The three of us would watch a contraction—a jagged mountain forming out of straight lines—come up on the monitor; then Morgan would take a big breath and push, while Trevor and I counted aloud to ten. It was a new feeling for me: watching my child give birth to her child. It made me feel connected to all the people who'd ever lived on earth.

When she pushed, I did too, until my own muscles ached. I last felt that ache in another San Francisco hospital back in 1978. When they placed Morgan, my first child, in my arms, pink and perfect, I thought that only professional ethics (not wanting to make the other new parents feel bad) kept the doctors from commenting on her unearthly beauty.

And here I was, twenty-four years later, when my first grandchild, Ryan Adair Anderson, arrived—black-haired, black-eyed, and perfect, her slanted eyes upside-down smiles. Through my tears I managed to find my camera and snap a digital image of her at the moment of birth.

That picture shows a wet little scrap of a thing, but just by arriving, Ryan profoundly altered everybody in her family forever. Morgan became a mother, Trevor a father. The other five of us became grandparents.

I became a grandmother.

## GRANDMOTHER 2.0

I was fifty-two. I thought that was so shockingly young—where was a kid like me going to find an apron and learn to crochet doilies on such short notice?—that I was astonished when I realized that my own grandmother, Dorothy, was fifty-two when I was born.

You could've knocked me over with a ball of yarn. That old lady? My grandma was a bit of a rake, with boyfriends, a job at Metropolitan Insurance in San Francisco, and a past as a member of the Women's Army Corps (my grandma really did wear army boots!), but by the time I was ten, she already had a white braid wrapped around her head and two Siamese cats wrapped around her ankles. She was *old*.

True, the average age women become grand-mothers remains steady, at forty-seven. But in the last century, the average *life expectancy* was forty-seven. Because grandmothers used to be old people, near the end of their shelf life, the stereotype is of a comforting human antique trailing a faint smell of lavender and strewn with cookie crumbs, grate-ful for any time or attention she gets.

We new grandmothers are not only not about to keel over dead—we're not even next in line. We have as much as thirty years of being grandparents ahead of us. And great-grandparents! There are going to be a lot of faces crowded around the crib.

People say to me, "You don't look like a grand-mother." As tactfully as I can, I say I *do* look like a grandmother—it's the picture of a grandmother inside their heads that has to be adjusted.

Grannies are all ages these days, ranging from thirties to nineties. Boomers have split down the middle, with some, like me, having their kids early and others just becoming empty-nesters. I had Morgan at twenty-six, which in San Francisco today is like having her at age nine (Morgan bucked the trend by having her first baby at age twenty-four). At one point, the average age for a new mother in San Francisco was over forty. At the swings, I can pass for one of the graying mommies nursing their babies while sipping no-fat, low-foam, decaf lattes.

Like those mothers, a lot of us grandmothers are in the middle of our lives and careers. And a grow-ing number of us are baby boomers, which as usual complicates everything. We are youth-obsessed, distracted by our careers, and vain. No one knows where Ryan got her almond-shaped eyes because she got them from me, and I had my eyes done in Bangkok. I imagine that many grandmothers with discreet procedures in their past have to hide a grin when they see that schnoz growing on a grand-baby's kisser. Shortly after she had become a grand-mother, Joan Rivers was told by the proud new parents that the baby had her nose. Rivers disagreed. "I didn't get this nose," she later explained, "until I was thirty-four."

In sum, we don't look much like the matriarch, monster, wise woman, fairy godmother, wicked witch, wolf bait, easily shocked geezer, or old lady eating cat food that the word *grandmother* conjures up.

Perhaps that's why I had *(ahem!)* a little trouble with what I was going to be called.

## MOP AND PLOP; OR, WHAT WILL THE GRANDCHILD CALL YOU?

> *Grandchildren don't make a man feel old; it's the knowledge that he's married to a grandmother.* —G. Norman Collie

I'd had nine months to choose a name to be called by when Morgan was pregnant the first time, and was no closer to finding one than when I started. I'd spent most of that time trying to avoid *Grandma*, a word that lay in wait for me like a pair of dentures in a glass.

It's the default word in my family: My mother is Grandma, and her mother was Grandma. My two older sisters are Grandma to their grandchildren. And Trevor's mother, Barbara, more mature than I am despite our being roughly the same age, cheerfully became Grandma, while his dad became Grandpa.

I couldn't be called Grandma, my husband, Bill, insisted, as if I'd told him it was my dream to be called that. He wouldn't sleep with a grandma; you couldn't make him. "Fine," I told him, "I'll get some-body else." But I understood. The word *Grandma* transformed his wife and Friday-night date into an old lady with graying hair that she hadn't found time to comb, oatmeal boiling on the stove, smiling uncertainly as Morgan dropped by in her business suit to hand over yet another squalling infant to go with the several others crawling on the floor.

As the months went by, I hadn't found another name. It was important. The name I chose would have a lot of responsibilities. It would have to allow me to claim Ryan as her grandmother—the person ready to open her fridge, her wallet, her house, and her heart to her. It would have to contain all the wonder of this new child in my life and all the wonder of watching Morgan find out, in her turn, the wonder of having a daughter.

And it would have to achieve all of this without giving me or anybody else the idea that I am old enough to be anybody's grandmother.

## WHEN THE BABY CHRISTENS YOU

Some grandmas like to leave their names up to the babies. Nana, Mimi, Boopsie, Yummy, Lovie. *Lovie!* Just shoot me now. These are names for lap-dogs, not human beings. (If that's your name, Yummy, I mean it in the nicest possible way, of course.)

I have a friend who went this route. One day she and her fifteen-month-old grandson came to the part in a storybook about the monkeys, and her grandson flapped his arms like a bird. She looked at him and said, "No!" Putting one hand on her head and the other on her belly, she told him that monkeys said, "Ou, ou, ou!"

And now that's her name: Ou-Ou.

Ou-Ou told me, "When you are given your name by a grandchild, it feels like being born again." But if the grandkid baptizes Grandma Ou-Ou, then Grand-dad is born again with something that goes with it—in this case, unfortunately, Poo-Poo. One grandmother became Mop, and her husband, naturally, became Plop. One woman was Big Momma, but the grandkids had trouble pronouncing Big Daddy, so their grand-father is Baggy. Big Momma and Baggy.

What about *Grandmother*, you ask? My mother-in-law has shown that even the tiniest tots can be taught to pronounce this name. But I couldn't take it on. If I did, I'd have to be the stately kind of grand-mother: you may kiss my hand, and have a look at the portraits of your forebears in the Great Hall, and here is a trust account for when you come of age, and isn't it your bedtime?

I needed a name that sounded more like me, an aging tomboy who can't cook and rides a bike every-where. I had good ideas vetoed. Jim, Morgan's father, is of Swedish descent, so I thought I could be Mor Mor, Swedish for "mother's mother." He could be Mor Far, "mother's father." Bill would be Step Mor Far. But everybody said that would be stupid and that we would all sound like characters in *Lord of the Rings*.

In exasperation everybody started calling me Nana. It felt to me like the verbal equivalent of being sent out on the ice floe when my teeth were too worn down to chew animal hides anymore.

Then, thankfully, Ryan dubbed me Baba, which is how her Russian babysitter referred to me. Morgan, who had begun to wonder if perhaps I didn't have the tiniest problem with being a grandmother, very nicely said "Bobbie" every time Ryan said "Baba," and in two days that was my name. (And no, Bill did not have to be Slobbie or Dobbie. He decided to be Pepe, like his own dad, who is French Canadian. And just in time, too, because we'd been calling him Faux Pas, as he is the stepgranddad.)

So what, you say. Who cares about any of that? She can call me anything she likes. I just want to see the baby. . . .

## IT'S NOT YOUR BABY

The Parent is in charge of who gets to see the baby. Yes, it's ridiculous; who would pass such a law?

I'm the grandmother! It's my natural right. How can I trust my grandchild with my daughter—someone who only five years ago threw up in the washing machine? Now I'm supposed to let her do whatever she wants with an *actual living being?*

Yes, you are.

After Ryan's birth, I went to see Morgan and Trevor, who live in a basement apartment three blocks from us in San Francisco.

Ryan was four days old. Neither of her parents had yet changed a diaper alone; they always did it together. "She's pooing!" Trevor would say, and they'd huddle around the baby, anticipating another excuse to change her clothes and marvel at her tiny knees. There was much discussion about whether the (far) overhead light was bothering the soundly sleeping baby. Finally, Trevor said, "Oh, I'll just hold her." When the hospital's home-checkup nurse came and asked, "Why is the baby so warm?" they had to admit that they hadn't put her down for ten hours.

I got to hold the baby after she nursed. Morgan gave me a cloth, not to protect me from spit-up, as I assumed, but so my sweater wouldn't irritate the baby. It had been a while since I burped anybody, but I was thumping away with a show of grandmotherly know-how when Trevor took her from me. "I know how to burp her," he said. I was surprised. His experience with babies, as far as I knew, was limited to having been one.

I stood back and watched. Still wearing his trademark ball cap, Trevor took his tiny daughter with confidence and a proprietary air. He patted her back, and a minute later, a loud burp announced the ending of an air bubble.

It was the beginning of a new knowledge for me: She was theirs. That's why they call having a baby "starting a family." They were a family, and I was not part of that inner circle.

I stole out of the flat and shut the door softly behind me. They needed to be alone with their baby. This is why, in the first weeks, when an extra hand may be desperately needed, the parents might try to do without you, or even hire a baby nurse instead. It's not personal, though it can feel that way to a grandmother who's cleared her calendar and had her bag packed for weeks.

Don't worry. If she doesn't want you to hold the baby, fine. It won't last. Wash the dishes or do the laundry. They don't know yet how important you are to their new little human.

You are the grandmother. You weren't a perfect daughter, god knows, and let's not even talk about you as a mother. Now is your chance to get it right. You can be a perfect grandmother.

Of course, you might not need any advice from me or anybody else. You might have a child who can breezily say, "I'm handling things, Mom. You don't have to worry about it," rather than get mad at you. Just as you might be the kind of grandmother who would never interfere, even when advice is backing up in you. If you are that mature, why are you reading this book? Please go away.

**Wait, did I say you can be a perfect grand-mother? Forget that. We know from being mothers what a setup that is—but you can at least be an up-to-date one.**

PART **2**

CHILD CARE
**Today**

## Parents Back When Dinosaurs Roamed the Earth vs. Parents Today

I was a kid in the 1950s. My mother had seven kids and got by with a playpen, a backyard, and a coffeepot. (I told her I couldn't believe she raised seven kids on her own, and by the way, why am I in a playpen in every picture?) We kids were set out in the yard in the morning and brought in at night, like cats. A kid who was in the house was a kid running up the light bill.

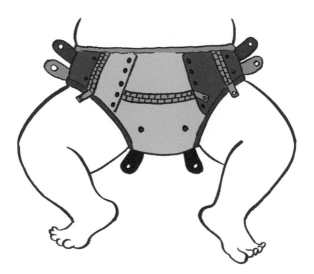

Back in the olden days, and even up through the 1980s, when Morgan and her brother, Patrick, were little, *parent* was a noun—something you *were*. Families were grown-up-centered. The kids followed adults around, jumping up to see over the dry-cleaning counter or trailing after the grocery cart.

Today, *parent* is a verb—something you *do*. Today's parents engage in an activity known as *parenting*. Adults follow kids around, from Gymboree to Music Rhapsody to Bright Child and Tumble Bugs. The rule that "children should be seen and not heard" has been tossed in favor of something like "children should be seen and heard and videotaped, photographed, and equipped with ID cards and reflective vests."

Baby powder has been eighty-sixed—gets in their lungs. Baby is nursed until she is old enough to unbutton your blouse. Toilet training lasts until the child herself gets tired of wearing diapers—even six-year-olds can still have a nighttime pull-up diaper. Playpens are out; babyproofing the house is in.

Today, the amount of mandated gear for a mother to pack for one baby's visit to the park will drop you to your knees: a bag full of diapers, an approved car seat, a stroller (you *can* collapse a stroller with one hand while holding a jam-covered infant with the other, can't you?), and sippy cups filled with water. The apple juice that we virtuously gave our babies is regarded with horror as empty calories. (It turns out tots can drink plain old water. Who knew?) Also, a cooler, a huge jug of water to rinse the baby's hands after the sandbox, plastic bags for disposal of diapers, extra clothes, baby wipes, milk, soy milk or lactose-reduced milk, and so on. You want to intercede and explain that the baby is not moving to the park but merely visiting it.

## SAFETY

When I was little, a seatbelt was Mom's arm— if I was lucky enough to be in the front. Otherwise, it was the back of her seat. Well, yes, we weren't buckled in, and we lived, etc., but we also fell out of cars a lot. (I remember my dad grumbling once when we had to go back half a mile to pick up my little brother Shannon.)

A near-fanaticism about child safety has set in since then. Not only the Parent but the child will refuse to let you turn on the engine until everyone is belted in. And not just the latch that goes across the chest: a baby of seventeen months will guide your hands to the intricate bottom latch if she suspects you were going to skip it this once. Get used to snapping, buckling, and then double-checking. We're talking about the most precious thing in your life, right? But weren't we precious, too, way back when? Although, statistically, danger from strangers is no greater than it was fifty years ago, kids don't leave the family premises alone anymore. A kid who has temporarily stooped down to gaze at Elmo in a shop window will straighten to find his distraught mother flagging down a police car.

The vigilance continues indoors. At Ryan's present preschool in San Francisco, the children are put in yellow T-shirts, escorted fifty yards down a corridor to a locked interior playground, escorted back, counted, and subjected to a roll call—all in a California state building you have to go through an X-ray machine to get into.

Useful hint: never tut-tut a safety concern, even if it's to suggest that a tyke riding a trike in a carpeted room skip the helmet just this once. Impress the Parent with your knowledge of the car seats voted safest by the Board of Hysterical Child-Safety Standards. Refuse to put the car in gear unless the kid is buckled in, even if the kid just finally fell asleep on the couch and now will have to be thrust into the car seat even though you're only going two blocks in a quiet gated community with speed bumps and you're driving a Volvo.

Never, never suggest that you leave a sleeping child in the car and just keep an eye on him.

## DO YOUR READING, OLD-TIMER

There have been changes since you raised
your kids, back when dinosaurs roamed the Earth.
Yes, it's annoying that the worried Parent flips
through *The Second Year of Life* and calls her pedia-
trician at 3 A.M. when you're right there to say a
little flat ginger ale will settle the baby's tummy. When
she rejects your advice, it can feel as if she's saying
that some of the things you did were wrong, such
as plunking the babies in the crib facedown. But,
in fact, it was wrong—your kids lived, as did mine,
but we were lucky, not right. Health information
changes every five seconds. It won't kill you to read
what your daughter is reading. Otherwise the
most well-intentioned comment might fall on deaf
(even sarcastic) ears. Case in point: When she was
a baby, Ryan had a bare spot on the back of her head
from sleeping on her back. Once, in a restaurant,
my mother warned Morgan darkly, "Her hair might
never grow back, you know." Morgan scanned the
room and dryly said, "You're right, Grandma. I see
a man over there who probably slept on his back

all the time." She pointed to a man with his back to us, his bald spot shining under the chandelier.

## LEARN THE LINGO

Today's emphasis on a child's self-esteem can look overly permissive to people who raised their children in the "Because I said so!" era. The very youngest kids play T-ball, a variation of baseball with, I think, no innings and no outs and no strikeouts—and they all get trophies at the end of the "season." Jumper castles and craft parties are de rigueur at children's birthday celebrations, which kick off at age one.

Also, modern parents avoid blanket praise. They don't want you to say "Good boy!" but to praise the specific action: "Julian, I like the way you picked up all of Grandma's court briefs and washed them in the tub." Kids don't do anything wrong anymore, but they often do things that are "inappropriate." Ryan, studying her feet—encased in pointy black dress shoes—from her car seat behind me as I drove her to school, remarked, "These shoes are inappropriate."

(She pronounced the word correctly, as if she'd heard it a lot.)

I said, "Then why are you wearing them?"

I glanced back to see her regarding her feet serenely. "They match my outfit."

A kid screaming incoherently because she wanted her Cheerios in the baggie with the pink rim, not blue, might hear; "Use your words, Abigail." Today, kids are given choices: "Do you want to climb into the crib by yourself or do you want to stay up all night watching old Robert Redford movies with Grandma?" (Kidding.) Choices can slow things down—a toddler can take a long time to choose a top, pants, shoes, and a jacket, and then more time must elapse while he or she is talked out of seasonally inappropriate choices or the lion suit left over from Halloween. Be Zen.

Kids are dressed like little adults—you see black dresses for toddlers. When I buy clothes for a six-year-old boy of my acquaintance, I follow his mother's cues and don't get him anything that his father wouldn't wear (e.g., no Spiderman themes). Toys play tunes and talk. Not just dolls—blocks, cars, and more. Walking past a toy box can set off a cacophony of tunes and little recorded voices. Even books read themselves when the kid pushes a button, so the parent can steal off for the last fifteen minutes of *The Sopranos*.

## THINGS THAT HAVE NOT CHANGED

Using all three of a child's names will still make him halt before running into the street.

Firmly stating "I'm going to count to three" still works (I don't know why, but it does).

# Don't Say Anything, Ever

Catching up on advances in child care is only the first step in staying on the good side of that bristly intermediary, the Parent. Following are more simple tips. (By *simple*, I mean simple for me to type, not simple for you to follow.)

Forgive me for telling you what you already know. Of course, you know better than to criticize. It's not as if you are a busybody, or a know-it-all. You don't intend to micromanage your grandchild's care. Just a word now and then when . . .

No.

*No what?*

No tiny suggestion that a baby with teeth a shark would envy might be able to manage a blueberry, no whipping out nail scissors to trim the baby's bangs, no suggestion that a baby is too thin.

*Can I . . . ?*

No. Not even little intakes of breath.

Yes, I know. You should be able to talk to the Parent without walking on eggs every minute, for heaven's sake. You changed the Parent's diaper, after all!

## EXACTLY WHAT NOT TO SAY

Carry this handy list in your wallet, so you'll know to avoid sentences that begin with such phrases as:

"You're her mother, but . . ."

"Shouldn't you . . .?"

"Won't he . . .?"

"Why do you . . .?"

"In my day . . ."

**Steer clear of utterances such as these, too:**

"We put you in the backseat on the floor
in a laundry hamper, and you loved it!"

"What's she wearing? What happened
to the red pants I gave her?"

"A little snack will do no harm."

"Does she really need that pacifier?"

"Her hair looks thin. Is she getting the right
nutrition?"

"Just turn out the light and tell her to go
to sleep."

"Why haven't you asked for my flash cards
so you can teach her how to read?"

"She'll lose that weight when she starts
to walk."

Why can't you just be your regular self, saying whatever comes to mind?

Because you can't.

You thought a hormone-crazed teenage daughter was touchy? Try a nervous new mother trying desperately to prove that she knows what she's doing. Anything you say (other than "Here's a check; no need to mention this to your father") will be wrong. When you say, "I want to help," she hears, "You're not doing it the right way." Even the sagest advice can come across as criticism, and criticism is hard for the Parent to hear from the person whose job it is to approve of her. She already suspects she's a bad mother because she can't figure out how to suction her son's nose with that strange bulb-syringe thingie. And she's not lying in a hammock, eager to swap parenting theories with you; she's tired, she's trying not to look at the sixteen unwashed sippy cups in the sink, and she's avoiding thinking about how cheese cubes have morphed into a major food group at her house. If you don't believe in her mothering skills, how can she?

Show her you do have confidence in her. Ask her how to do things. Pretend that you have never picked up an infant before. Ask your daughter how to tape the diaper snugly so it doesn't leak. Marvel at the new engineering of diapers.

Praise her. "That's wonderful that you let the baby crawl around the house and develop her curiosity instead of putting her in a playpen. Can I borrow all the stuff on your floor?"

Praise how patiently she helps her child to the correct behavior ("Your feet belong on the floor, honey"). Admire how your grandson says please when he asks for orange juice and how easily he accepts that he can't have the red balloon (and get rid of the balloon. They're now regarded as a choking hazard, as you know from your reading).

Stand around silently exuding confidence. It may comfort a new mom just to be around someone who has enough perspective to know that very little causes permanent harm, except neglect. The near-hysterical anxiety that typifies the mother–child bond is on the whole absent in the grandparent, and thank god for that. You know that the colicky baby is gonna get over it and that the world won't come to an end if the child eats dessert first and then dinner.

Grandfathers seem to get in trouble with remarks about names; grandmothers, about hair and clothes.

## NEVER CRITICIZE THE PARENT'S CHOICE OF NAMES

Whatever they name the kid, you love it.

"We've decided to call the baby Onree, spelled phonetically."

"I love it!"

"We've decided to name him Herman Bertha, after his other grandparents."

"Perfect!"

And no nicknames. For some reason, Morgan refused to let me call Ryan "Bingo," which I started doing after I took her as a baby to a Sisters of Perpetual Indulgence bingo game. So I stopped. I should never have started: I've spent the last twenty-six years trying to keep my son Patrick's name from being shortened. (When his friends call, I say there's no one named Pat at this number.)

## DO NOT SAY ANYTHING ABOUT YOUR GRANDCHILD'S HAIR

This rule remains in force even if she has on her head:

(a) Nothing.

(b) A Scotch-taped bow calling attention to (a).

## DO NOT SAY ANYTHING ABOUT WHAT YOUR GRANDCHILD IS WEARING

Even if your grandchild appears in plastic high heels three sizes too big and a tutu over her baby sister's pink pants, you can't take it for granted that she dressed herself. Neither should you conclude that your grandchild's outfit of a purple dress over corduroy pants decorated with teddy bears is meant to be a riff on the 1960s or a slap at the other grandma's taste (if the other grandma is the source of the corduroy pants). Always assume the outfit was chosen by the Parent and adjust your remarks accordingly. Just say, "I'll look for the other high heel."

## WHAT ABOUT STEALTH ADVICE?

Can you buy a guide to toilet training and leave it on the table where the Parent usually puts her diaper bag down?

You can, but try to be out of range. Even a paperback can hurt if flung across the room.

Neither can I recommend sending a clipping, with a cheery "FYI!" note attached, about a baby who developed frostbite because her mother was carting her around in too few layers.

You can, however, get a friend to mention to your daughter in passing how cute the toddler's hair would look in a pixie cut (as opposed to streaming down all sides of her head).

## DOES IT COUNT IF YOU SAY IT TO THE BABY?

"Oh, is Sweetie Pie cold? Does Sweetie Pie wish she had longer socks?"

You're welcome to try addressing to the baby remarks you don't dare make to the Parent, but you risk hearing the Parent address the same little personage in a similar singsong: "Does Sweetie Pie wish Nana would go home and take her irritating widdle remarks with her?"

## DON'T KNOCK THE FATHER, NANNY, IN-LAWS, OR MOMMY'S FRIENDS, EITHER

Disapproval of anybody the Parent chose to have in her life, right down to the dry cleaners she picked, is interpreted as disapproval of her. So don't risk it.

## BESIDES, WHY GET IN TROUBLE FOR NOTHING?

It's not as if she'll *take* your advice. There's no record in human history of an adult child saying, "You're right! I should keep the baby from chewing on speaker wire! The scales have fallen from my eyes! Thank you, wise mother!"

Did she follow your advice when she was fourteen and not buy those Fayva platform shoes? "But Mom, they're only $19!" With a trip to the ER, X-rays, and a cast, didn't those shoes end up costing $543?

# Spot Quiz

**Let's see if you have been paying attention.**

**1**

Your grandchild appears to have been taken straight from the crib to the car seat without a detour to the place where the hairbrush is kept.

YOU SAY:

A. "I think I have a brush in my purse somewhere."

B. "I always took the trouble to make sure you looked nice."

C. "Looks as if we may get a little rain."

Answer: C

You are on the phone with the Parent. You have recently heard about random kidnappings and want to tell the Parent immediately. You just hope it isn't too late. Can you casually interrupt the Parent to ask if the baby is still in her crib?

A. Yes
B. No

Answer: B

(You get extra credit for not running over to see for yourself.)

The grandchild howls because her sweater is buttoned wrong (by you, no doubt—time to buy the drugstore glasses in the 3.00 strength). The Parent informs you that there are seven kinds of crying and tells you which kind this is.

YOU:

A. Laugh until you yourself are demonstrating one of the seven kinds of crying.
B. Ask where she read that and ask to borrow the book.

Answer: B

## WILL THE DAY COME WHEN I CAN SAY WHATEVER I LIKE TO MY DAUGHTER, AS I WOULD TO A NORMAL PERSON?

No.

But your tact will not go unnoticed.

A friend told me, "My mother has always had a hands-off approach when it comes to my children. We were living in my parents' house when Justin was born. Even so, when I was deciding to breast-feed or not, and when Justin was screaming his head off with colic, she showed me that she trusted me to look after the baby, and I appreciated that. She allowed me to seek out help when I wanted it. She was concerned, but she was not intrusive."

## BUT I'M WORRIED! I HAVE TO SAY *SOMETHING*

Of course you're worried. You can't love a person without worrying about her. There's a balance to be struck between bombarding the Parent with unwanted advice and being the extra pair of eyes and ears that every grandkid and her mother benefit from.

Being a member of the bite-your-tongue club doesn't mean you have to sit there for the next forty years with duct tape across your mouth.

If you really need to say something, say it. But pick your moments—you can't take those words back. Calm times when nobody's mad and the grandkids are not present work best.

## REFRAME THAT REMARK

Did you get to where you are in your career by just blurting stuff out? No. Be diplomatic. Spend a few seconds spinning those criticisms into observations instead.

Sharing your own experiences will make you sound less like a know-it-all. Morgan was having daily morning tussles with Ryan, who doesn't like to have her hair brushed and has to be threatened with being left behind just to get her into a coat. I told my daughter that discipline never came naturally to me. "I couldn't even get a thin plastic bottle away from a fifteen-pound baby," I said casually as we stuck stars to the ceiling of Ryan's room. It's true, too—when Morgan was almost two, I was still getting up at night to change her soaked diaper, sleeper, and blankets and all but wring out her mattress. If there had been hotels for babies, I would have called her a cab.

 **1** Don't say, "I dressed her in something warmer." Instead say, "We were talking about the colors of the rainbow, and I got out her green jacket to show her."

**2** Don't say, "You never do what you say you're going to do! How's a kid going to learn?" Instead say, "I am not sure if this would make a difference or not, but I always try to follow through on my warnings. I noticed that you told William to finish his beans or he can't watch *Rolie Polie Olie* on TV, but there are the beans, and he's watching the show."

 **3** Invoke the experts she is always throwing at you: "When a child will eat only cold tortellini, Dr. Smarterthananygranny recommends . . ."

## ANNOUNCE THAT YOU HAVE SOMETHING ANNOYING TO SAY AND ASK FOR PERMISSION TO SPEAK

Step up to the mike, take a deep breath, and begin. "Kids, these are your children, and I don't want to interfere. I just want to tell you my opinion, with the understanding that you don't have to listen to me." And then say, "You probably haven't noticed, but Seth listens when you and Stephen argue about who was flirting with whom at the bar, and you may want to make sure he's out of earshot the next time the two of you . . ."

The Parent will bristle, but stepping back, not wanting to intrude, can make a grandma less vigilant when her experience is needed. Case in point: My sister Robin's three-year-old daughter, Katie, was walking around a family backyard barbecue in just a pair of shorts. My mother kept staring at her and remarking, "There's something wrong with that child's chest." That's the kind of grandmother remark everybody tends to ignore, but Mom kept saying it. Katie's left clavicle protruded more than the right. Robin took her to the doctor (maybe just to shut my mother up), and Katie was successfully operated on for a hole in her heart a month later.

I wished I'd been as alert as my mother after Maggie—Morgan's second child—was born. I was being so great at not intruding that I didn't notice Morgan was hurting more than is normal following a birth. She attributed it to walking the three blocks to my house, and I accepted that, though at the back of my mind I remembered walking a mile round-trip to the hardware store the day after my ten-pound son was born (stupid, I know). Morgan ended up in the hospital with a dangerous uterine infection that should have been caught much earlier—and I wished

I had been a bit more insistent that she get her pain checked out.

## THE WAY NOT TO ASK FOR PERMISSION TO SPEAK

"Now, darling, you won't get upset if I say a little something, will you?" (This is a good way to let her know that you are about to say something obnoxious, probably about hair, and that if she objects, she's oversensitive.)

## WAYS TO SPEAK UP WHEN YOU ARE SAFELY AT A DISTANCE

E-mail is good. They can digest (seethe over) your remarks at leisure, and you're at a safe distance away from them. I like to start with a generous pre-amble designed to remind Morgan that I help out as well as offer tips: "Hi, sweetie! Just dropped the kids off," or "When cleaning up after my weekend with the girls, I . . ."

Once I wanted to say something to Morgan about Ryan's school. I hated how the kids and even teachers at two-year-old Ryan's institution of lower learning just stood here and there on the wood floor when I dropped her off, with no one talking, presumably because school hadn't officially started yet. Ryan cried when I left her, the rims of her eyes smudged pink with distress in a way that made my heart drop into my shoes.

So I e-mailed Morgan. I started by saying, "Just back from dropping Ryan off. I wonder if it's time to look for another school . . ."

Morgan, pregnant again, with Maggie, and in law school, was all tight-lipped resentment. "And where is this other school?" she wrote back. "Who's going to do the research to find it?" But she'd noticed the same things, and a week later, she transferred Ryan out of the Stepford School of the Stunned.

In truth, the Parent is no dummy and will feel pounced on whether you send your two cents on e-mail or spray-paint it on the house. Luckily, spats are short. If you get accused of meddling, despite your efforts at diplomacy, this might be a good time to note that the grandmother who never meddles is a grandmother who's taking tango lessons in Argentina. Would the Parent like a mother who is as slow to help as she is to hinder?

PART **3**

FACE TIME WITH YOUR
**Grandchild**

# Babysitting

The Parent may be especially bristly because she needs a break. She daydreams about being blissfully alone with a toasted peanut butter and jelly sandwich, a bottle of red wine, and a six-inch stack of unread *New Yorker* magazines or copies of *InStyle*. Offer to babysit while the child naps so she can take a walk. If she's a stay-at-home mom, that goes triple. Hand her an MP3 player and sneakers, and tell her not to come back for at least two hours—and stress that she'd better have wine, or at least coffee, on her breath when she returns.

Her kitchen may not be familiar to you if you live out of town, but why not make some meals while you're there and fill the freezer? A full fridge is a godsend at 5:30 P.M. when the rat patrol is ramming your ankles with trains and cars.

My friend Linda said one of her nicest memories came when her mom visited after her second son was born. "Mom ordered me to take a nap and told me that she and Max, then three, would work on supper. I remember lying in bed, not really sleeping, listening to them chat in the kitchen while Mom made rice and chicken and salad. Mom asked Max who his best friend was. I heard Max say, 'Nathan.' 'What do you like to do with Nathan?' Max talked about rockets and dinosaurs, with Mom responding in all the right places. I peeked out and saw him standing on a chair next to her while she washed lettuce at the sink, and I flashed back to doing the same thing with her when I was small."

Giving the Parent a break means you get your hands on—I mean help out with—your grandchild. This is a fine thing. But it brings us to the subject of babysitting, an activity that gives you oh so many new ways to mess up.

## AT YOUR HOUSE

You have two options for preparing to have your grandchildren at your house.

**1** Do nothing. Spend their visits snapping at them not to touch the crystal vases, swooping up pill bottles off bedside tables just ahead of the curious tot, lunging at falling lamps, and watching raspberries being ground into your sixteenth-century Persian carpet. This will give you needed exercise and keep you mentally alert.

**2** Make some adjustments. Study your house from the point of view of a reckless little guest who will happily put anything in his or her mouth, climb anything, apply food to any surface, and wash paperback books in the toilet. Crawl around at baby level until you have identified and dealt with all the hazards, like that innocent floor lamp and its sinister partner, the cord. That shiny toaster on the counter? Keep it unplugged unless you're using it. Pad the edges of your glass coffee table, remove the knobs from your stove (and try to remember where you put them), put a lock on the toilet, and get a gate for the stairs. And what about that swing-out cabinet for plastic bags? *Plastic bags?* What are you, some kind of loon? You can't have plastic bags in your house! Take them out to the trash right now. While you're out there, cement in the pool.

Make your house welcoming to grandkids as well as safe for them. Buy toys, plastic dinnerware, cheese sticks, and a little table for them to eat at. Put up lots of pictures of them. Ryan was barely past one when she began noticing the pictures of herself on our walls. My husband bought one of those stainless refrigerators that you can't stick anything to, and I'm still mad at him. A refrigerator is good for keeping food cold, but its main purpose is to act as a display medium for kids' drawings.

I turned Morgan's old bedroom into a playroom, but please note: I do not recommend going this far. Now I'm dragged in there within minutes of the girls' arrival and forced to build towers of blocks for kids who think it's hysterical to knock them down. I'm made to dress Polly Pocket dolls (Ryan likes to outsource her doll dressing) and take the roles assigned me in games. I have to be the baby, or be the mommy, and lie down because I am sick. I say, "What if I don't want to be the baby? Can I be the mommy instead?" and Ryan, who has been told not to be bossy, puts it another way: "You be the baby, OK? And I be the mommy, OK?"

## AT THEIR HOUSE

When you arrive and are waiting for the Parents to go out, act like what you are: a guest. Avert your eyes from the diapers spilling over the pail in the bathroom. Do not open the fridge. Do not let your hand idly sort through the *(unpaid!)* bills, unreturned videos, or bedside medications.

Do not clean their house. If you *do* clean their house, don't surprise them with the baggie of marijuana you found under the couch, and don't ask why you have to use only Tom's of Maine organic toothpaste while they can leave controlled substances on the floor.

Stay out of the Parent's bedroom. You were not allowed in there when she was a teenager, and you aren't now, unless you know for sure that the orange tennies that go with your retro brown and yellow jogging suit are in there, in which case a quick sprint in and out is allowed.

## FOLLOW THE PARENTS' RULES

You will be tempted not to. Unlike parents, grandparents are not judged by how their grandkids turn out. Nobody says, "Didn't your grandmother teach you *anything*?"

No wonder we get on the Parents' nerves. We have the easier job. My mother—seven children, thirteen grands—had phone conversations with her mom friends in which they counted up the trips to Europe, wardrobes, and careers they missed out on while they were slaving over a stove to feed kids who would, despite all this nutrition, grow up too weak to pick up the phone or pull a Mother's Day card from the rack. So, why did they have kids at all? they asked each other. The answer was always the same: to get to the grandkids.

And no wonder. Giddy with relief that you are not responsible for raising these tots but only for entertaining them until the Parent gets back, it's easy to behave as if you have been assigned the role of FunMom. You can make them scream with laughter by writing all over them with washable markers, and give the Parent the role of the spoil-sport who insists on scrubbing them off. You can give the kids pizza for breakfast or pancakes for dinner. Why not? Mean old Mom can force down a little steamed broccoli later to make up for it, tra la.

Not fair. Remember when you were the Parent and picked up the overtired, sticky, cranky kidlets; drove them home; forced a vegetable down their Popsicle-stained throats; threw them protesting into the bath; and made them go to bed—all the time listening to them yell about how they want to go back to Grandma's?

I sure do. "Oh, wasn't she supposed to have that?" my mother would blink innocently when I'd pick up Morgan and find chocolate all over her face and her tuna sandwich untouched.

Since you already have all the joy of kids without the day-to-day grind, be a sport. Follow the Parent's rules. Laugh at the nine-page letter from the Parent if you like, but read it. (For one thing, it will tell you how to work the TV.) Here's an actual excerpt from a note Morgan left me: "Press grey DVR button, go down to *Rolie Polie Olie*, and press select. If she goes pee-pee *(not poo-poo only)* in the potty, she gets a butterfly—in the blue cupboard. Sometimes she has to poop right at bedtime—she will want to go to the potty even if she already pooped in her diaper. She uses the big potty with the little one as a step stool. The bedtime routine picks up where it left off."

## IF A RULE IS IMPORTANT TO THE PARENT, THEN IT IS IMPORTANT TO YOU

"Here, let me slather you with sunscreen, even under your clothes, so you won't get sunburned on our trip out to the mailbox at the end of the driveway."

Even the Parent who does not want to tell you what to do with your own grandchild in your own house may make a point of mentioning the child's skills—scraping her plate after dinner, dressing herself, going to sleep promptly when put to bed at 8 P.M. sharp. Pick up on such hints. A Parent has a routine calculated to produce a well-fed, well-behaved, happy child who goes to bed on time. Reassure her that you will follow the schedule the kid is used to.

## IF YOU DON'T FOLLOW THE RULES, HAVE AN EXPLANATION READY

If that under-caffeinated day-care teacher tells the Parent the two of you habitually arrive late for school with goofy expressions and the tot misses the entire discussion of ellipsoidal rectangles, smile disarmingly and say:

> ◇ You went three blocks out of your way because the air quality on the usual route seemed a tad below standard.

> ◇ You stopped by the Highway Patrol office to have the car seat checked out again, just in case.

Do not divulge to the Parent the real reason(s):

> ◇ You decided to dye eggs although Easter was a month away.

> ◇ *Someone* has to pet the lonesome goldfish at the pond at the Japanese hotel.

## DO NOT SULKILY FOLLOW THE RULES WHILE MAKING IT CLEAR TO THE GRANDCHILD WHOSE POOPY RULES THEY ARE

Don't say, "Mommy says no, you may not have the dolls with feet that snap right off so you can change her shoes."

Don't say, "It's up to Mommy" when you know any mommy worth her baby wipes will veto a stick of Doublemint at 8 A.M.

## DO NOT WHINE

"One Popsicle won't hurt him, sweetie."

"Does he have to go to bed so soon?"

## YOU BE THE HEAVY FOR A CHANGE

Don't say: "Mommy said you can't have a lollipop, and Mommy is the boss."

Say: "I don't want you to have a lollipop. Candy isn't good for you."

Don't say: "Mommy said that all toys go into the toy box at bedtime."

Say: "It's pretty clear, Adriatica. No noisy or pointy things in your bed. The police whistle and the backhoe gotta go. That's it."

When your grandchild tears price tags off in the store after everybody told her not to, declare, "That's a time-out for you." Watch the Parent's happy face when *le petit criminal* runs to her for protection from mean Grandma instead of the other way around.

While we're on the subject, before you pick up a crying, hiccuping grandchild and offer to beat up whoever upset him, find out if he has been reprimanded by his mother.

## WAYS TO DISCIPLINE
## A GRANDCHILD

A child who blows bubbles in her milk must be rushed into the bedroom and thrown on a heap of pillows as a punishment.

A child who won't allow her hair to be brushed must be chased around the kitchen with the brush until her giggling slows her up enough for her to be caught.

If she puts her Jell-O in her hair and waits solemnly for you to react, invent an errand in an adjacent room, go there to laugh, wait until you think you can manage a glare, and come back and help her clean the Jell-O off. *(Practice alone until you're sure you can bring this off.)*

### BEDTIME

If the Parent says two picture books and a short made-up story are the perfect bedtime fare, do not convert this to reading four books, telling two stories out of your head about a reluctant dragon slayer and a sarcastic dragon, and jumping on the bed, followed by you squeezing into the crib to watch her eyelashes flutter as she sleeps. (Besides, begin as you want to proceed: How you put her to bed will become how she wants to be put to bed, every time. Babies are more conversant with precedent law than lawyers.)

## FEEDING YOUR GRANDCHILD

Follow the Parent's rules about food, right down to the way she wants the grape skinned and cut into quarters. There is no wiggle room in this area.

**1** If you slip the kid Count Chocula cereal, chicken nuggets, or pizza, or, god help you, a Happy Meal, by current parenting standards you may as well be running a crack house. In fact, do not hand an item of food to any child under ten unless you have asked the Parent *(OK, I'm exaggerating, but you get the idea).*

**2** Do not allow the child to lick the jam off the bread.

**3** Even if you have to go across town to the Whole Foods store and pay six times as much for it, buy the brand of baby food on the list the Parent gave you. If the Parent says organic milk, buy organic milk.

## IF ICE CREAM IS AGAINST THE RULES, DON'T GIVE YOUR GRANDCHILD ICE CREAM

And if you *do* give her the tiniest taste of ice cream, spare the Parent the knowledge of this teensy slipup. Check the baby's mouth and clothes and your sleeves for traces before the Parent arrives. (Don't forget about the spoon in the sink.)

## MEMORIZE THIS SENTENCE

"I have no present recollection of how the ice cream got in the baby's mouth."

## DENY, DENY

In the absence of incriminating digital photographs, swear you're innocent.

Parent: "Austin's got ice cream all down the front of the clothes I just put on her. What did you give her?"

You: "Nothing. Your real daughter is in the other room, clean and full of organic cereal. Oh, my god, whose baby is this?"

If you buy the child Cheetos, and congratulate yourself that you had baby wipes in your purse to erase the evidence, do not spell out the child's name on a bench using Cheetos and then take a digital picture of the result. It will be found.

You might be caught even when you've cleaned away all traces, as I was when Maggie ate an orange I gave her, and Morgan found a large peel in Maggie's tattling diaper. In such cases, I like to go straight to the over-the-top apology: "I can't believe I gave her that after you told me not to. I am a horrible grandmother," etc., etc. Wring your hands. Allow her to comfort you.

*(Obviously, don't ask, "Why can't the baby have an orange, for Pete's sake?")*

# Not Babysitting

*The years between fifty and seventy are the hardest. You are always being asked to do things and are not yet decrepit enough to turn them down.* —T. S. Eliot

It's likely you weren't sitting somewhere with your hands folded, hoping the phone would ring, when a grandchild entered your life. Grandchildren get added to a long list of demands on your time. They are time-consuming. And it's not as if they were your idea, right?

Did anyone ask you before going ahead and making you a grandmother? No. You're a bystander. You were subpoenaed.

They're not yours.

By the time you have a grandchild, you might finally be at the point where you don't have to rush home. You can take that cruise, write that book, compete in the Sunfish Championship, or go off on the Harley. You are about to make CEO, or you have a lot of other obligations—aging parents, younger children still at home, volunteer work. Then along comes a new little burden, I mean, bundle of joy.

When I couldn't take off work to help after Maggie's birth, Morgan was disappointed. "I know you're busy, Mom," Morgan said. "But I can't help wishing you could help more. I thought that was what grandmothers did."

I felt my heart lurch. Who doesn't still believe, at heart, that coming right over to help is what grandmothers do? Grandma bakes cookies and baby-sits, while Grandpa builds a dollhouse. I was a busy staff writer at a newspaper, a job I'd held for sixteen years, but still waves of guilt and regret at not being available swept over me.

The self-sacrificing grandmother as a cultural construct has us all in its grip. We have few models that show Granny checking her BlackBerry and saying she hopes she can make Christmas but can't be sure.

It's not only that we feel we *should* pitch in. We want to. The instinct to help may be built into our genes. It's said that only when Grandma and Grandpa became available to care for the children were Mom and Dad freed up to invent the wheel, agriculture, and bronze.

And we are one of the few species in which females do not go on reproducing for the entire life span (a trait we share with, ahem, elephants and whales). There's a "grandmother hypothesis" that says menopause is linked to grandmothering: We stop being able to have children ourselves so that we can give a grown child with young children crucial help with hers.

But, hey, don't feel guilty. "Send me a postcard, Grandma!" the grandchild says as you snap your suitcase shut and head out the door. "Both my parents work, but my babysitter can drive me to swim class . . ."

Just kidding. Of course, you're going to feel guilty. Today's granny wants to work, wants to play, and wants to throw clay, all in the same twenty-four hours. She wants to get that report done, and she wants to use exactly those same minutes to go for a walk with the baby, especially as she knows how quickly the baby will grow, while work will always be there.

This feeling may be familiar from back when you had to choose between bringing the cupcakes to school and making it to the regional meeting. But that doesn't make it easier. How do you feel if you've been promising yourself for forty years that you'll write that novel when you retire or when the last kid leaves the house, and instead you spend every waking moment shopping for the baby, sitting with the baby, or talking to the baby's mother about the baby? Whatever a woman is doing, there's always something else she should be doing.

Once again you have to choose, and once again you know that whatever you chose, you lose something of incalculable value. That's the way the cookie (bought on the run, not homemade) crumbles.

If your grandchild is a new stick to beat yourself with for not doing enough, try what self-help books suggest—find a quiet moment to talk to the Parent about what you expected, what she expected, what help she would like, and what help you can give. Make a date for the sole purpose of such a talk, so she can't change the subject. Buy her an expensive lunch. Urge her to order wine. Then, lean forward and use those skills you learned on the job. Negotiate.

Tell her that you can't be the kind of grandma she needs you to be without giving up some things important to you, but you will do what you can. Tell her caring for the baby does not, these days, always include taking care *of* the baby. "I'm not willing to give up my writing or my traveling," you can say, "and I won't be able to show up at every game or holiday event or birthday party. But I'll be available in emergencies, and I will spend time with them when it's just them and me, and they'll know I'm there."

Once you make promises, though, don't let the Parent down. When I'm late picking up Ryan, Morgan feels she can't say anything, because I'm so busy and still trying to help. But not being able to count on me being where I say I will be makes her feel as if she doesn't have the support she needs.

Just be clear. If you don't want to be a regular babysitter, don't. Nobody likes a martyr. And day care can be wonderful; it really can. Ryan and Maggie thrive at their school, where spirited and well-trained young child-care workers talk about the stars and butterflies and let them paint the paper and each other with spray bottles and teach them to share nicely with the horrid other children, none of which they would get at home with a grandma about to blow her brains out if she has to play "You be the mommy and I'll be the baby" one more time.

The Parent won't stop wishing you could spend more time with them than you do, and you might not either. But if I've learned anything by being a grandmother, it's that both the Parent and the grandchild will feel loved when they see you in there trying.

# What You *Can* Do

Today's grandma may no longer be the one grown-up who has loads of time, but she *may* be the one grown-up who has loads of money (thanks to that job that keeps her from being able to babysit). Cash is as welcome to strapped young parents as advice is not. They say that the money used to go up: You helped your grandparents. Nowadays, the money often comes down. Most of us grandparents today are better off than we thought we would be, and our kids are worse off than anybody expected them to be. My kids can afford the high cost of living in San Francisco because their dad and my husband and I own the building they live in (which explains my luck in having my two granddaughters only three blocks away).

Many of us have hand cramps from writing checks: slipping money to the parents for rent and down payments, private schools, saxophones, and La Petite Baleen swim classes. A friend told me that she recently realized her grandmother paid her way through college. She hardly noticed at the time— "I need to go, somebody has to pay, after all"—but now she knows, and she flies east twice a year to see her grandmother.

It behooves Grandma, by the way, to be all the more careful not to throw her imposing self around when providing financial support. "I'm grateful for the help," said one mother whose in-laws pay for private school and summer camps. "But it makes it harder to say no when they ask us to visit or do things with them. It's as if they're calling the shots in our lives."

One right you have is to slip into baby stores with a grandmotherly gleam in your eye. One day when Ryan was a baby, I met Morgan down the block in Duboce Park after work. As I pulled a doll and a toy cell phone out of my backpack, a woman watching nearby drawled, "Let me guess. This is the grand-mother, and it's the first grandchild."

If you can afford the Playskool kitchen and the Parent can't, this is a perfect way to let the grandchild know who loves her more.

Just kidding. Buying things for the grandkids requires tact. It's best to clear big presents with the Parent, even if this denies you the big splashy surprise entrance carrying a three-story dollhouse with a working kitchen. The Parent may not want her to have it or may wish you could chip in on the diapers as long as you're such a big spender. (This may be true for what you buy the Parent, too: Morgan just asked me to exchange the two suits I got her for Christmas for toilet paper, diapers, and baby wipes.)

No, cheapskates, you don't have to have your pocket picked just because you're the grandmother. If you are not the type to buy elaborate presents— or if you have no money, or if you can hardly open the door of the child's room without being buried under cascading Polly Pocket cruise ships, Robo-reptiles, pink CD players, and miniature plastic strollers—then bring her an old piece of costume jewelry or a magnifying glass. Loot the backyard for twigs for trees and the toy box for little cars and make a town out of Play-Doh. Give her an imaginary horse to keep in her room, as I did Ryan. Generously, I even let her pick the color. ("But I still want a real one," Ryan said patiently as she went along with the pretend pink horse.)

## PRESENCE

Savvy grandmothers know hours logged is the kind of expenditure that registers with tots. A childhood filled with wonderful memories of time spent with Grandma is a better inheritance than a bank account. (Depending on the grandma and the bank account, of course—your results may vary.) Even if you don't have endless stretches of leisure, you can make the time you have with your grandkids count. After all, kids never used to spend much time with their granddads, but they have warm memories of them anyway. Funny thing about grandmothers—everything we do, the kid remembers. My friend Rose cherishes a memory of the day her grandmother came into the dining room kicking her leg up and turning her foot in tight little circles in the air. She danced right up to Rose and taught her the cancan. "By the time I was fifteen, we had a chorus line, my cousin, grandmother, and aunts, and we'd cancan through the house after the dishes were done," Rose said.

## PASSING DOWN YOUR TICS AND ODDITIES (I MEAN VALUES)

Studies show that as many as nine out of ten adults feel their grandparents influenced their standards and morals (yes, for the better, smarty-pants).

"My role is to teach Sky about what I value," says Marin poet Anne Hansen. She is spiritual, and the parents are not, and this is what she wants to pass to her grandchild. In addition, Anne has a standing date on Wednesday afternoons with Sky. "We hang out for the whole afternoon. I take her to dance class. Yesterday I rented a violin for her and taught her a little about bowing. We go to Indian restaurants and have *mag lassi*."

Teach your granddaughter how to sit quietly in a beautiful church or how to make kites out of funny papers—and when to let the wind take the kite and when to reel it in. Drag that grandson from his computer and show him how to smell the air for rain. Astound him with the information that there was no color TV when you were born and that you had to walk all the way across the room (in the snow)

to change the channel. He'll shudder and shoot you a sympathetic look.

Show them your world. I do not always take Ryan and Maggie straight to the park. Parks are boring. A big, undeserved time-out for Grandma. (Besides, the slides are so slow they might as well make them horizontal and be done with it.) I take them on the streetcar, to the mall, to friends' houses, to the bookstore, or to discover the luminescent light on a San Francisco beach in December—wherever I'm going myself. Besides, the best talks happen in the car, even though you are bombarded with difficult questions, such as why did you give that man on the bridge five dollars and why is your hair red now and would you rather be eaten by a shark or a grizzly bear?

Kids love to work, being at this age unable to distinguish it from play. You might get them to give you a hand. If I'm painting a container for the garden, then the girls and I paint (they use water). Everybody has fun, plus I've managed to get around the child-labor laws and save a few bucks.

It used to be that you went to visit Grandma or she visited you. But today's souped-up version of Grandma doesn't bond by sitting around burping after dinner; she bonds on the way to the planetarium, on a camping trip, while lacing up in-line skates, at a rock concert. Helena Koenig, owner of Grandtravel, told me, "I know when I open a newspaper and see that a theater group is in town, my first thought is which grandchild to take to it. When my kids were little, I couldn't afford seventy-five dollars for a theater ticket! I had five kids. I never could take them to restaurants. But now, my husband and I, every time we get in the car to go someplace, we are saying, 'Gosh, we should get so-and-so. He would love it.'"

Not the Energizer Bunny type? Let the other grannies whiz by on their Trek road bikes with a tot in a matching helmet on the back. What's the matter with being the one to read them a book? (No, not *Anna Karenina* in the new translation.) This is especially true if your daughter waited until her forties to have kids, and you got a trifle creaky (in an interesting way) during that delay. You may have to sit through *Finding Nemo* instead of that new French flick, but afterward you can talk about fathers and children. Or, you know, fish.

PARENT, SCHMARENT:
# You and the Kid

PART **4**

You follow the Parent's wishes about the daily routines, but otherwise your relationship with this tender little ur-human is your own, and you and the kid get to make the rules for that. One grandson trails bits of toast all over his own house, but at Nana's house, he eats at the table. "The rule is no one can get up from the table, once we sit down," his grandmother told me.

## Grandmothers Who Fly

Most grandparents live a lot farther than over the river and through the woods from their grandchildren—for some it's over the continent and through the crowded airport terminal to baggage claim. The disadvantages are plain: You aren't there for her preschool solo in *The Wiz* or his first dive. You can't stroke the new baby's impossibly smooth skin or feel her weight on your lap. One grandmother lamented, "I couldn't be there for the first weeks, and that's when they get your smell." You can't see the growing child and pick up what his expression and his body language say that the phone calls and e-mail don't. And they in turn lose the Proustian "smell memories" that come with going to Grandma's house.

On the other hand, you get to be a romantic Auntie Mame. The visits are more intensely anticipated

and more vivid for being rare. Who doesn't remember the weekend or week alone with grandparents, feeling like a royal child? One grandma whose two grand-daughters live across the country was despondent at first at missing so much, but now she enjoys the regular travel. Flying has made the world so much smaller that many grandmothers think nothing of getting on a plane to spend a couple of days and create a relationship with a grandchild. Summer Kircher will fly practically anywhere for her grandchildren. A garden designer from Colorado Springs, Colorado, this grandmother of four drives seventy miles to Denver every week to see her granddaughter and one year flew to Iowa six times to visit her son's two boys. She even took one grandchild to Italy.

In between, there's e-mail, Webcams, letters, and more. One grandma made videotapes of herself reading aloud to her grandsons with a little drama thrown in. When she reads *Charlotte's Web*, a spider falls through the air next to her on a fishing line. She wears a fireman's hat to read a book about firemen. (I'm not sure how long she's prepared to keep up the tradition; it might be hard to arrange the burning of Atlanta behind her for the camera while she reads *Gone with the Wind*.)

If you can't be there in person, be there on the wall. Get the Parent to put a picture of you where the kid sees it a lot. Maybe dress it for the different holidays. Look, a lei! Grandma's in Hawaii this week. Make sure the Parent talks you up. "You know, Grandma has red shoes like yours." Consider using a theme, too. For example, if you're from Texas, fill the kid's house with items from Texas—longhorns or oil wells or whatever you have down there.

## THE PAYOFF

Whether you live across the street or across an ocean, whether you have short, sweet visits with your grandkids or see them every day, your attentions to your grandkids pay off for you as well as for them. Many grandmothers report that this role offers the in-the-moment experience they missed as harried young mothers. It's a second chance to relish the fleeting days of childhood. When her two daughters were born, Kathy Gold was twenty-eight and thirty, respectively, and trying to make her way in the world—finish med school, get a job, and be a wife. Now, with her grandchild Ethan, she says, "I let my work leave my head, and I am just with Ethan, whereas with my own kids, I saw that stage as more of an obstacle—something to get through so they could become independent. I took care of Ethan for five days when his day care was closed, and I thought this was as close to meditation as I would come. I wasn't thinking of past or future, only the immediateness of feeding him raisin toast and drawing roads on butcher paper in the exact places he demanded they should go."

English grandmother and writer Nell Dunn echoed this when she wrote of her grandson, "What Cato gives me is the sheer pleasure of living. He reminds me that there isn't so much to it all, that actually a good breakfast, a nice walk, a new word, good weather, a new hat, can be outrageously delightful, and all those things that take enormous effort are not necessarily where our satisfaction comes from."

Grandkids bring you into a sweeter, slower present. They show you the future at a time when a lot of your friends are thinking about the past. And they take you back to childhood—theirs, the Parent's, your own: a three-time admittance to a wonderland. (Depending on the childhood, I know. Leave me alone. I'm allowing myself a sentimental moment.)

They remind you of the pleasures that reside in memory. One morning Ryan and I pedaled to Golden Gate Park (in the opposite direction from her school—*shhhh*) to see if the blackberries were ripe yet. Very few were, and those had been mostly plucked clean by the other berry lovers who got there before us. I showed her how to check the undersides of leaves to find overlooked berries. As I did, I remembered picking blackberries with my mother and then how I poured milk and sugar over them. They tasted so good I couldn't stand still but had to walk up and down the brick-patterned linoleum floor eating them. I ate blackberries with Ryan, and I was nine years old again.

## Besotted

> *When a child loves you for a long, long time, not just to play with, but REALLY loves you, then you become Real. . . . Generally, by the time you are Real, most of your hair has been loved off, and your eyes drop out and you get loose in the joints and very shabby.*
> —Margery Williams, *The Velveteen Rabbit*

> *If nothing is going well, call your grandmother.*
> —Italian proverb

Every new grandmother you talk to appears to be on drugs: "Why didn't anybody *tell* me it would feel like this?" Sharyn Fox thought the most miraculous moment of her life was when she awoke after laser surgery on her eyes and could see the acacia trees outside her bedroom window. "How wrong I was!" she says. "Six months later I became a grandmother and learned what the word *miracle* really meant."

When I became a grandmother myself, I couldn't find any books about grandmothers that didn't make my teeth ache—they were just all so *sweet*. I figured out why: It is difficult to write about a family relationship that seems to offer a lot of uncomplicated, well, joy. The birth of a grandchild reduces your basic female to a happy, drooling idiot.

I am so happy to have the little ankle-biters around that I have to insult them just to keep things from getting sloppy. "Cantaloupe head!" I say to Ryan. "Blueberry butt!"

"Sandwich foot!" she hollers back up at me.

I look down at her haughtily. I am not a sandwich foot. I am a mature woman with mortgages and responsibilities. I put her in her place with an elegant riposte. "*You're* the sandwich foot!"

I call her the hall monitor and tell everyone she'll be the office weenie when she grows up. Though still only three, she's always telling me to put things back, park closer to the curb, give Mommy back her shoes, or not give Maggie a ball so small she can put it in her mouth. The other day she picked a yellow circle out of her multicolored Froot Loops and held it up to me: "We're only supposed to have this color, Bobbie," she said sternly. (But she ate the other colors, I noticed.)

What about you? Have you not only started a blog about your grandchild but launched it well before birth, with the ultrasound pictures? Did you tell that famous novelist seated next to you at dinner that your grandson waves to his penis when he's getting a diaper put on and says "Bye-bye" in a regretful kind of voice?

We're all besotted. But try to get a grip. The mature head of an international conglomerate reduced to gibbering ecstatically about how one of her grandson's toes always gets left outside the sandal is not a pretty sight.

It may be time to get things back in perspective. Call your friends; look up the listings of plays. Get your *New Yorker* and *Harper's* magazines from underneath the stack of *If You Give a Pig a Pancake* books, and read them. Go to a café or bookstore (or, hell, a bar), and sit there for an hour or so. Avoid sitting near any moms or kids. Read a book or magazine and remember how you walked around in your pre-grandmother skin almost perfectly.

## THE MANY DRAWBACKS OF GRANDCHILDREN

**A reminder of the ways in which grand-children are unsatisfying companions for a woman of your accomplishments may help you collect yourself.**

### BABIES

◇ Once you've seen them asleep and then with their eyes open, you have seen the whole act.

## TODDLERS

◇ They have way too much stuff, and their stuff is plastic and brightly colored—not at all what you had in mind when you did the living room in the Japanese minimalist style.

◇ They're too short. You get a crick in your neck talking to them. If you pick them up, perhaps to give them your thoughts on their not-well-thought-out shortness, they take your glasses off your face—even though they've been told a million times, "No! No! Oh, you did it again!"

◇ Their English is atrocious even though they've been in the country *their whole lives.*

◇ The younger ones poop in their pants *all the time*—not just accidents.

◇ And when was the last time a toddler asked you a question about yourself? I gave Ryan a children's board book I published and said *tres* casually, "I wrote that." I patted the book meaningfully. She looked at me. She was too polite to put the book down, but you could tell she was thinking about it.

◇ A youngster always has his hand out. "Hand me that sippy cup, doll face." But does it go the other way? Hardly.

◇ They freak out when you take a tiny bite of the bagel *that you bought them.*

◇ Their nerves are shot—they pitch a fit when you absentmindedly use their pirate kerchief to wipe your glasses.

And what do they give you? Grandchildren are famous for pawning off amateurish works made of egg cartons and Scotch tape in lieu of more meaningful gifts, such as checks. And the reason they don't write checks is that they don't work. Not even part-time. They don't want anybody else to work either. If you make a stack of blocks, they'll knock it down. If you read a magazine, they will draw on the page you're on or pour all their toy trains into your lap. The sight of a grandma even glancing at a laptop sends them into a frenzy of lap climbing so they can type the *R* they know their name starts with.

They kiss you so hard your face hurts. And they don't say hello but immediately run to get something to show you, as if they have instantly assimilated the delight of your being there, like a little stream of happiness coursing through them.

## LOOK AROUND

While you're trying to gain perspective, you might notice that there seem to be other people in your life. There's the man you're married to. You might recognize him as the one who got stuck with the Earth, Wind & Fire tickets because you told your daughter the two of you would love to babysit Friday night.

And who's that slumped over a geometry textbook next to him? You may still have younger children living at home. Politeness requires you to continue to pay these other members of your family the occasional small attentions, even when your grandchild is present.

## WHO'S THAT WITH YOUR GRANDCHILD?

My own mother didn't even try to keep up a decent show of interest in us, her actual children, as the grandchildren came along. I suspect she thought of us as the grandkids' drivers. She kept a freezer filled with Popsicles, baskets overflowing with toys, and dressers stuffed with kiddie clothing, but if my sisters and I wanted a Coke, she reminded us the store was down the road, first turn to the left. "And bring back some crackers and juice for the kids."

You can do better than she did. Remember to direct a remark or two to the grandchild's driver, especially if you are pretty sure the driver is someone you gave birth to. Before you lunge for the grandkid, show some interest in the Parent: admire one article of clothing *("Is that a new blouse?")*, and ask one question about work *("Are you still a lawyer?")*.

Remember that unless you are lucky enough to marry someone who already has grandchildren, your children are indispensable in the production of these magical beings. Not to mention that, chances are, they're the ones who will be picking out your rest home.

THE PATERNAL GRANDMOTHER AND

# Cutting Grandma Some Slack

PART

# The Auxiliary Grandmother

Ryan and Maggie have another set of grand-parents (Bob and Barbara), which means they have, most pertinently, another grandmother. Trevor is Bob and Barbara's only child, and Ryan and Maggie are their first grandchildren, too. They are around our age, but both have retired early. They knock together cradles, bought Ryan a miniature Hummer that goes by itself, and say things to Morgan and Trevor such as "Come live free in our house!"–the poor things, as if their roles are anything but distant, pathetic shadows of mine.

The other grandparents are the auxiliary grand-parents, kept in storage in case of need. (My friend Carol confides she doesn't even like the photographs the other granny takes—"They make the kid look corn-fed and common.")

The mother of the Mother is *the* grandmother. As I read somewhere, the mother of a daughter who gives birth to a daughter is the closest kind of grandmother you can get.

Yes, I have a son, and I plan to have a more evolved view by the time he has a child. In the meantime, I'm the grandmother in these parts.

If you are the mother of a Father, I imagine that besides having to put up with attitude in the mother's mother, other things are different for you. You may not be as tempted to get on the Parent's nerves with a lot of advice (her mother is taking care of that). Besides, you can talk to your son.

Trevor says his mother never gives him specific advice, but she will say things like "Don't be overbearing; let her be who she is; understand that she's three." I asked him how he feels about his mother's comments. "Thankful," he said.

Fathers are cool. The Father will cheerfully let you criticize the way he dressed his baby and what he fed it. He will not flip out if you object to your granddaughter being put to bed in the clothes she wore all day. (He will tell the daughter-in-law what you said, but at least you didn't have to be there.)

As the mother of a Father, however, you must have problems of your own, right? Sure, you don't have as much prickly history with a daughter-in-law as a mother has with her daughter. But, as you may have picked up from my snarky remarks above, you may feel as if you are the grandma of another family's baby—that you are building close relationships of which you are not in control. If you don't get along with your daughter-in-law, or she is not comfortable letting you have the kids on your own, there's not much you can do. Should the couple break up, the Mother's mother is all the more involved, while the Father's mother may find herself out in the cold along with him.

With the national divorce rate running at 50 percent, this alone is a reason to forge a good relationship with your daughter-in-law. Barbara threw Morgan's baby shower, bringing her friends and all the party trimmings down from her home in Davis to do so. Morgan finds her easygoing, uncritical, and helpful: Barbara babysits anytime she is needed. The two of them go shopping alone, without Trevor along. She will always be Maggie and Ryan's grandmother, no matter what.

Not the more important one, of course. That would be who, again? Oh, yes. Me.

## Cutting Grandma Some Slack: A Note to the Parent

Dear Parent,

Please forgive your mother for asking you to cast an eye over these few pages, but she did just read a whole book telling her how not to blow it with you. I want to urge you to be patient with her, to let her make mistakes while she adjusts and figures out the rules. We grandmothers often really don't know how you want us to behave. For example, because my husband, Bill, and I have friends our age with kids three and six who throw the kids at us and run at breakneck speed out the door whenever we visit, I thought I was helping Morgan when I took Maggie from her, but it felt to her as if I was grabbing the baby away from her.

I needed time to figure out when to step forward and help, and when to step backward and do and say nothing. Making this more complicated is that our maternal instincts are triggered by the new baby, just as yours are. When the baby cries, a grandmother's instinct is to pick him up; she has to learn to let you do it. I remember a time when I helped Morgan get ready to take the kids to the park on a chilly January, and she looked over and said, in a casual tone that didn't fool me, "Did you throw the kids' jackets into the stroller because you assumed I would not have thought of jackets for them?"

My mouth dropped open. I muttered something about how of course I knew she would have a jacket for them, but then I felt myself trailing off, confused. The real answer was that the last time I felt this strongly about two small children, they were mine.

It was my role to soothe them, feed them, and keep them warm. I automatically imagined icy drafts on their pale, soft necks and saw to it that they had jackets. I knew (if I had thought about it) that Morgan always had what she needed for the kids, but she's my child too. It was all I could do not to tie a jacket to the stroller for her, too (I did hang a muffler around her neck).

I know it's hard to be patient when your mother races you to the crib and has more baby furniture than you have (not to mention gained a whole cup size in sympathy with you when you were pregnant). It's even harder when she gives you support that undermines you—tucking a bottle into the diaper bag on a shopping trip when you are trying to breast-feed or telling you to let the child cry herself to sleep. My own mother babysat her grandkids generously, but there was always a steady barrage of remarks to ignore: Why is she dressed like that? Why don't you cut her hair? Oh, for heaven's sake, just put her on her tummy, or she'll flail about all night. It was trying to listen to—but worth it, as my kids feel strongly connected to their grandmother.

Remember, that grandmother is your mother, and she's just trying to help. Talk to her about what you expect, and what she expects, and try to notice the good stuff. A grandmother who bought your child noisy green and pink clogs that the day-care teacher had to write a note about is a grandmother who went into a store, pondered choices (those boring white tennies, formal black Mary Janes, or those cool clogs?), bought the crazy clogs, and looked forward to presenting them. The exasperating grandmother who kept the child up an hour past bedtime, leading a parade of noisemakers through the house or drawing the giggling kid in chalk on the kitchen floor, is also, if you squint, the mother who skipped work to stay with your child when you had to go out of town. If you remind yourself to remember these things, you may feel gratitude rising to the surface: It's hard to go on feeling resentment toward someone when you're setting up a portable crib in her spare bedroom as you get ready for your child-free sprint to warm Hawaiian sands. She may forget to hug you as she lunges for the ankle-biter, but then, somehow, the hug she gives your child seems to magically land on you, too.

# Afterword

PART **6**

Wouldn't it be nice if reading a little book could turn you into a perfect grandmother who always says and does the right thing? Alas, if little books worked, we would all be thin and rich and wise. And if you think this is an awful lot of advice from someone who does not actually have a Ph.D. in grandmothering, or is not even a particularly good model, you can at least be grateful that I took the trouble to go ahead and do some preliminary blundering for you.

I saw a cartoon once of a mother leaning over a crib, looking at her baby girl and thinking, there they were, all the mistakes waiting to be made. The same cartoon could show you and your grandchild.

**Go forth and screw it up. Forgive yourself. Try again.**